# WOULD YOU RATHER?

## CHRISTMAS EDITION

### COPYRIGHT

# WOULD YOU RATHER...

SPEND A DAY WATCHING CHRISTMAS VIDEOS

OR...

SPEND A DAY CHRISTMAS SHOPPING AT THE MALL

SEE THE NUTCRACKER

OR...

DANCE IN THE NUTCRACKER

# WOULD YOU RATHER...

BE ONE OF **SANTA'S** ELVES

## OR...

BE ONE OF **SANTA'S** REINDEER

GET MANY SMALL PRESENTS FOR **CHRISTMAS**

## OR...

GET ONE BIG PRESENT FOR **CHRISTMAS**

# WOULD YOU RATHER...

BE GIVEN $100 FOR
CHRISTMAS TO BUY THINGS
FOR YOURSELF

## OR...

BE GIVEN $1000 BEFORE
CHRISTMAS TO USE TO BUY
GIFTS FOR OTHER PEOPLE

---

RECEIVE SOCKS FOR
CHRISTMAS

## OR...

RECEIVE A DICTIONARY FOR
CHRISTMAS

# WOULD YOU RATHER...

VISIT THE NORTH POLE

## OR...

VISIT BETHLEHEM

HAVE A JOB WRAPPING PRESENTS AT THE MALL

## OR...

HAVE A JOB TAKING PICTURES OF CHILDREN SITTING ON SANTA'S LAP AT THE MALL

# WOULD YOU RATHER...

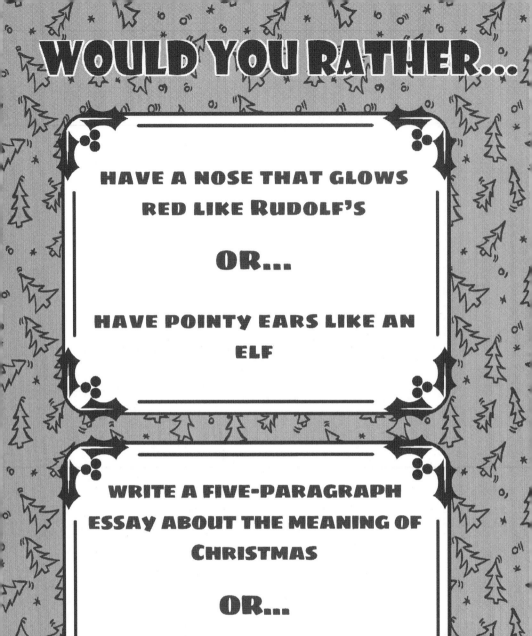

HAVE A NOSE THAT GLOWS RED LIKE RUDOLF'S

## OR...

HAVE POINTY EARS LIKE AN ELF

WRITE A FIVE-PARAGRAPH ESSAY ABOUT THE MEANING OF CHRISTMAS

## OR...

SOLVE A PAGE OF CHRISTMAS-THEMED MATH PROBLEMS

# WOULD YOU RATHER...

BE ALLOWED TO ONLY EAT FRUITCAKE FOR TWO DAYS

OR...

BE ALLOWED TO ONLY EAT CANDY CANES FOR TWO DAYS

LIVE IN A GIANT GINGERBREAD HOUSE

OR...

RIDE ON THE POLAR EXPRESS

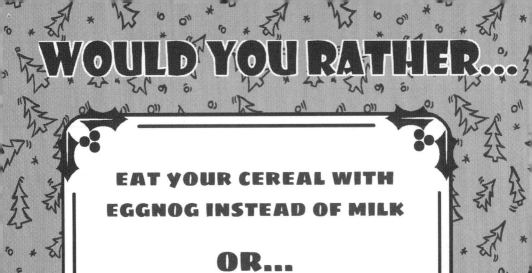

# WOULD YOU RATHER...

EAT YOUR CEREAL WITH EGGNOG INSTEAD OF MILK

## OR...

EAT A CANDY CANE SANDWICH

BE AT HOME ON CHRISTMAS AND GET LOTS OF PRESENTS

## OR...

GO TO DISNEYLAND FOR CHRISTMAS BUT NOT GET ANY PRESENTS

# WOULD YOU RATHER...

HAVE CHRISTMAS TREE TINSEL FOR HAIR

OR...

HAVE FINGERNAILS THAT LIGHT UP LIKE CHRISTMAS LIGHTS

---

HAVE MISTLETOE HANGING IN YOUR BEDROOM DOORWAY

OR...

HAVE A LARGE, DECORATED CHRISTMAS TREE IN YOUR BEDROOM DOORWAY

# WOULD YOU RATHER...

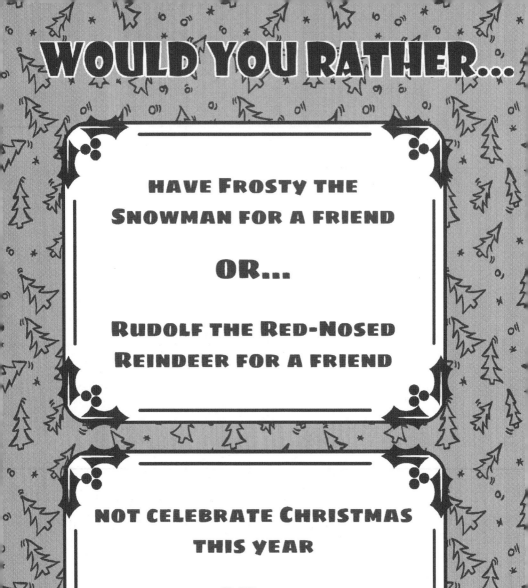

HAVE FROSTY THE
SNOWMAN FOR A FRIEND

OR...

RUDOLF THE RED-NOSED
REINDEER FOR A FRIEND

NOT CELEBRATE CHRISTMAS
THIS YEAR

OR...

NOT CELEBRATE YOUR
BIRTHDAY THIS YEAR

# WOULD YOU RATHER...

MAKE PRESENTS FOR YOUR FAMILY INSTEAD OF BUYING THEM

## OR...

MAKE ORNAMENTS FOR YOUR CHRISTMAS TREE INSTEAD OF BUYING THEM

HAVE TO LOUDLY SING THE CHORUS OF "JINGLE BELLS" EVERY TIME YOU WALK INTO A ROOM FOR A WEEK

## OR...

HAVE TO WEAR A SANTA SUIT TO SCHOOL EVERY DAY FOR A WEEK

# WOULD YOU RATHER...

GO FOR A RIDE IN SANTA'S SLEIGH

OR...

GO FOR A RIDE IN LAMBORGHINI

EAT CHRISTMAS DINNER AT HOME

OR...

HELP SERVE CHRISTMAS DINNER TO THOSE WHO ARE LESS FORTUNATE

# WOULD YOU RATHER...

## WEAR SANTA'S RED SUIT TO SCHOOL

### OR...

## WEAR A GREEN ELF SUIT TO SCHOOL?

## WORK IN SANTA'S WORKSHOP

### OR...

## WORK IN A GIANT TOY STORE

# WOULD YOU RATHER...

HAVE A SNOWY CHRISTMAS

OR...

HOT CHRISTMAS, WITH NO SNOW AT ALL

DECORATE 100 CHRISTMAS TREES

OR...

DECORATE 100 CHRISTMAS COOKIES

14

# WOULD YOU RATHER...

LOSE YOUR VOICE FOR THE HOLIDAYS

OR...

ONLY BE ABLE TO SPEAK IN CHRISTMAS CAROLS

BE BEST FRIENDS WITH FROSTY THE SNOWMAN

OR...

BE BEST FRIENDS WITH RUDOLPH THE RED NOSED REINDEER

# WOULD YOU RATHER...

OPEN YOUR PRESENTS ON
CHRISTMAS EVENING

OR...

OPEN YOUR PRESENTS ON
CHRISTMAS MORNING

BE ALLOWED TO LISTEN TO
CHRISTMAS CAROLS FOR A
YEAR

OR...

HAVE TO MAKE TOYS FOR A
YEAR

# WOULD YOU RATHER...

DRINK ONLY EGGNOG ALL December

## OR...

EAT CANDY CANES ALL December

CHRISTMAS CAROLING

## OR...

GO SLEDDING

# WOULD YOU RATHER...

BE A MOUSE AND RECEIVE A BIG PIECE OF CHEESE FOR CHRISTMAS

## OR...

BE A CAT AND RECEIVE A BIG FISH FOR CHRISTMAS

WEAR SANTA'S BIG BOOTS TO GYM CLASS

## OR...

WEAR POINTY ELF SHOES TO GYM CLASS

# WOULD YOU RATHER...

BE A MELTING SNOWMAN

OR...

BE A MUNCHED ON
GINGERBREAD PERSON

MAKE TOYS ALL YEAR LONG

OR...

PLAY WITH TOYS ALL YEAR
LONG

# WOULD YOU RATHER...

HAVE TURKEY FOR
CHRISTMAS DINNER

OR...

HAVE A HAM FOR
CHRISTMAS DINNER

SPEND A DAY WITH MRS.
CLAUS

OR...

SPEND A DAY WITH SANTA
CLAUS

# WOULD YOU RATHER...

EAT **CHRISTMAS COOKIES**
WITH **SANTA**

**OR...**

BAKE **CHRISTMAS COOKIES**
WITH **MRS. CLAUS**

EAT A GINGERBREAD HOUSE

**OR...**

LIVE IN A GINGERBREAD
HOUSE

# WOULD YOU RATHER...

BE MRS. CLAUS

## OR...

BE THE HEAD ELF IN SANTA'S WORKSHOP

HAVE A BELLY THAT SHAKES LIKE A BOWL FULL OF JELLY

## OR...

EAT A BOWL FULL OF JELLY

# WOULD YOU RATHER...

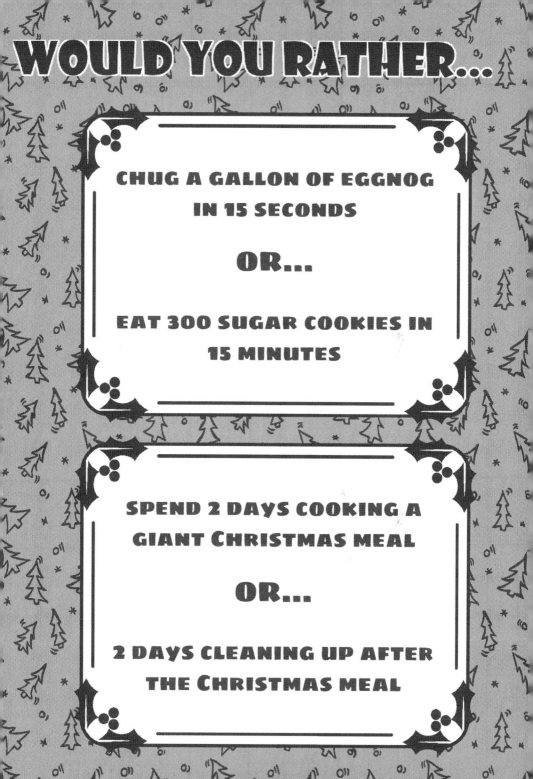

CHUG A GALLON OF EGGNOG IN 15 SECONDS

OR...

EAT 300 SUGAR COOKIES IN 15 MINUTES

SPEND 2 DAYS COOKING A GIANT CHRISTMAS MEAL

OR...

2 DAYS CLEANING UP AFTER THE CHRISTMAS MEAL

# WOULD YOU RATHER...

NEVER EAT CANDY AGAIN

## OR...

NEVER PLAY IN THE SNOW AGAIN

LIVE IN A GIANT GINGERBREAD MANSION

## OR...

BUILD A GIANT GINGERBREAD MANSION

# WOULD YOU RATHER...

BE ONE OF SANTA'S WORKSHOP ELVES

## OR...

BE A 13-INCH WALKING TALKING NUTCRACKER FOR THE REST OF YOUR LIFE

LIVE IN A GIANT GINGERBREAD MANSION

## OR...

BUILD A GIANT GINGERBREAD MANSION

# WOULD YOU RATHER...

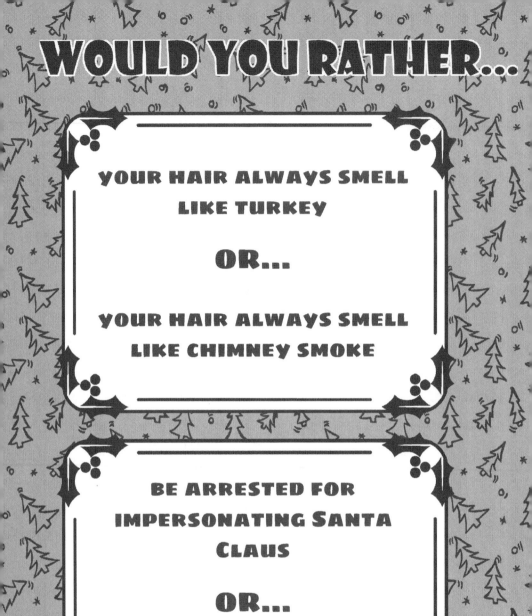

YOUR HAIR ALWAYS SMELL LIKE TURKEY

OR...

YOUR HAIR ALWAYS SMELL LIKE CHIMNEY SMOKE

BE ARRESTED FOR IMPERSONATING SANTA CLAUS

OR...

BE ARRESTED FOR STEALING PRESENTS

# WOULD YOU RATHER...

EAT A CHRISTMAS DINNER
THAT'S COMPLETELY
COVERED IN CRANBERRY
SAUCE

## OR...

GRAVY SAUCE

NEVER HAVE HOT
CHOCOLATE AGAIN

## OR...

NEVER WATCH A CHRISTMAS
MOVIE EVER AGAIN

# WOULD YOU RATHER...

GIVE ONE PERSON A $1,000

OR...

GIVE 1,000 PEOPLE A $1 GIFT

HAVE ELF EARS FOREVER

OR...

SANTA'S WHITE BEARD
FOREVER

# WOULD YOU RATHER...

SIT IN A TUB OF HOT
CHOCOLATE FOR 6 HOURS

## OR...

TRY TO STUFF 100
MARSHMALLOWS IN YOUR
MOUTH

STAR IN THE WORLD'S
WORST CHRISTMAS MOVIE

## OR...

DRESS AS MRS. CLAUS FOR A
YEAR

# WOULD YOU RATHER...

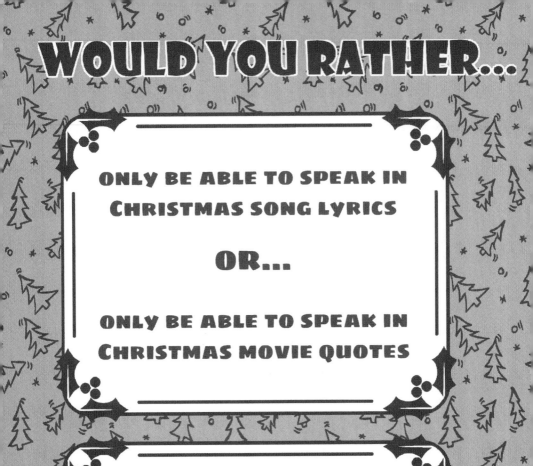

ONLY BE ABLE TO SPEAK IN CHRISTMAS SONG LYRICS

OR...

ONLY BE ABLE TO SPEAK IN CHRISTMAS MOVIE QUOTES

HAVE CHRISTMAS DECORATIONS UP ALL YEAR

OR...

NEVER BE ABLE TO PUT THEM UP AGAIN

# WOULD YOU RATHER...

SHOP FOR 2,000 GIFTS

OR...

WRAP 2,000 GIFTS

HAVE SANTA CLAUS SNEEZE
IN YOUR FACE

OR...

HAVE A REINDEER POOP ON
YOUR SHOES

# WOULD YOU RATHER...

CELEBRATE CHRISTMAS EVERY MONTH

OR...

ONCE EVERY 10 YEARS

SING CHRISTMAS SONGS SOLO TO AN AUDIENCE OF 2 MILLION PEOPLE

OR...

WET YOUR PANTS WHILE SITTING ON SANTA'S LAP?

# WOULD YOU RATHER...

HAVE CANDY CANES FOR FINGERS

## OR...

GUMDROPS FOR EYES

GIVE YOUR CRUSH A THREE-YEAR-OLD FRUIT CAKE

## OR...

A PAIR OF USED CHRISTMAS SOCKS

# WOULD YOU RATHER...

READ A 2,000-PAGE BOOK
ABOUT CHRISTMAS

## OR...

WRITE A 2,000-PAGE BOOK
ABOUT CHRISTMAS

---

KISS A POLAR BEAR

## OR...

KISS A COMPLETE STRANGER
UNDER THE MISTLETOE

GET ACCIDENTALLY LOCKED
IN THE MALL

## OR...

STUCK AT THE AIRPORT ON
CHRISTMAS

HAVE A BIG BELLY LIKE
SANTA CLAUS

## OR...

HAVE A BIG GLOWING RED
NOSE LIKE RUDOLPH

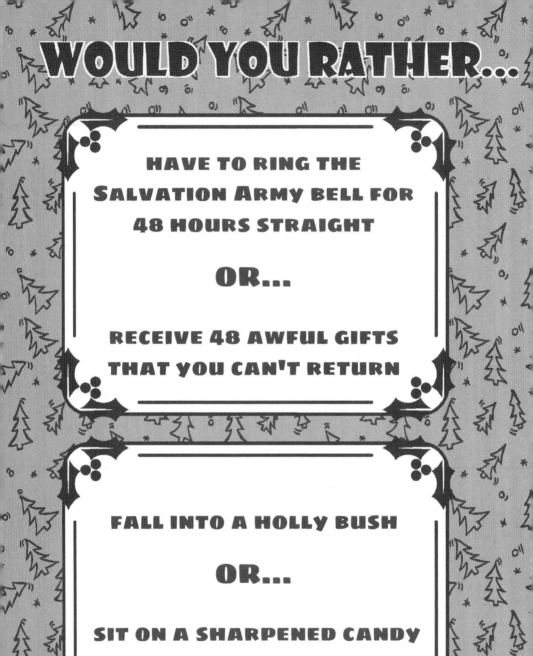

HAVE TO RING THE SALVATION ARMY BELL FOR 48 HOURS STRAIGHT

OR...

RECEIVE 48 AWFUL GIFTS THAT YOU CAN'T RETURN

FALL INTO A HOLLY BUSH

OR...

SIT ON A SHARPENED CANDY CANE

# WOULD YOU RATHER...

HAVE SKIS FOR FEET

## OR...

TINSEL FOR HAIR

---

DECORATE YOUR HOME WITH
CHRISTMAS GARLAND MADE
FROM SOMEONE ELSE'S DIRTY
UNDERWEAR

## OR...

DECORATE YOUR TREE WITH
WET CAT FOOD

# "WOULD YOU RATHER...

ACCIDENTALLY BREAK THE WORLD'S MOST EXPENSIVE CHRISTMAS TREE ORNAMENT

## OR...

STEAL SANTA'S SLEIGH

BE COMPLETELY ALONE

## OR...

HAVE 100 PEOPLE CRAMMED INTO YOUR HOUSE ALL CHRISTMAS DAY

# WOULD YOU RATHER...

BE TURNED INTO A REAL DONKEY FOR A NATIVITY PLAY

OR...

SING JINGLE BELLS VERY LOUDLY FOR AN HOUR IN A LIBRARY

HAVE 11 PIPERS PIPING

OR...

12 DRUMMERS DRUMMING

# WOULD YOU RATHER...

WALK BAREFOOT ON A MILE-LONG PATH OF LEGO BLOCKS TO GET EVERYTHING YOU'VE EVER WANTED FOR CHRISTMAS

OR...

THROW AWAY 10 OTHER PEOPLE'S PRESENTS TO GET EVERYTHING YOU'VE EVER WANTED FOR CHRISTMAS?

KNIT A SWEATER MADE OF SANTA'S BEARD HAIR

OR...

WEAR A SWEATER MADE OF SANTA'S BEARD HAIR

# WOULD YOU RATHER...

BE PERMANENTLY COVERED HEAD TO TOE IN FUR

## OR...

HAVE ANTLERS THAT FALL OFF AND GROW BACK EVERY YEAR

EAT A MASHED POTATO AND CANDY CANE SANDWICH

## OR...

WALK AROUND THE MALL WITH MISTLETOE OVER YOUR HEAD FOR 3 HOURS

# WOULD YOU RATHER...

SPEND AN ENTIRE DAY UNTANGLING CHRISTMAS LIGHTS

## OR...

SPEND AN ENTIRE DAY OVERCOOKING CHRISTMAS COOKIES

LOSE ALL OF YOUR LUGGAGE

## OR...

LOSE ALL THE GIFTS YOU BOUGHT AT THE AIRPORT

# WOULD YOU RATHER...

HAVE A CARROT FOR A NOSE

OR...

REINDEER HOOF HANDS

LAUGH 'HO HO HO!' AS YOUR USUAL LAUGH

OR...

HAVE A HIGH SQUEAKY VOICE LIKE AN ELF

# WOULD YOU RATHER...

BE THE ONLY PERSON TO NOT RECEIVE A GIFT

## OR...

BE THE ONLY PERSON THAT GAVE GIFTS

BE KRAMPUS

## OR...

BE THE ABOMINABLE SNOWMAN

# WOULD YOU RATHER...

HAVE EGGNOG FLAVORED FRUITCAKE

OR...

FRUIT CAKE FLAVORED EGGNOG

HAVE A TALKING CHRISTMAS TREE THAT NEVER STOPS TALKING ABOUT TREE STUFF

OR...

HAVE A LIT FIREPLACE THAT NEVER GOES OUT

BE IN A PRODUCTION OF THE NUTCRACKER

## OR...

RUIN A PRODUCTION OF THE NUTCRACKER

GET STUCK IN A CHIMNEY FOR FOUR HOURS

## OR...

WEAR A DIFFERENT UGLY CHRISTMAS SWEATER EVERY DAY FOR FOUR MONTHS

# WOULD YOU RATHER...

HAVE TO WRITE SANTA'S 'NAUGHTY OR NICE' LIST

## OR...

HAVE TO CHECK THE LIST TWICE FOR HIM

DECORATE AN 80-FT TALL GINGERBREAD MAN

## OR...

BAKE A 1-TON FRUITCAKE

# WOULD YOU RATHER...

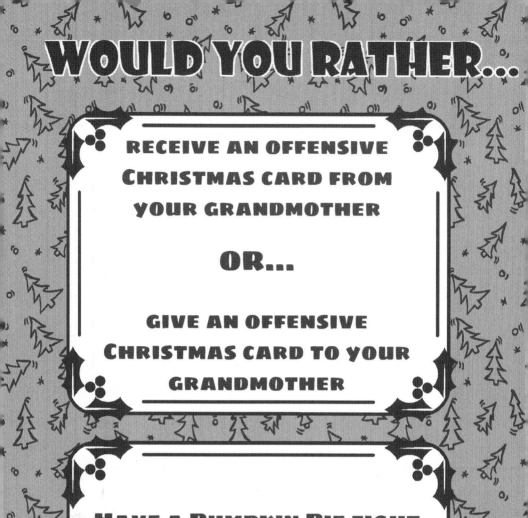

RECEIVE AN OFFENSIVE CHRISTMAS CARD FROM YOUR GRANDMOTHER

OR...

GIVE AN OFFENSIVE CHRISTMAS CARD TO YOUR GRANDMOTHER

HAVE A PUMPKIN PIE FIGHT

OR...

AN APPLE PIE FIGHT WITH FRIENDS

# WOULD YOU RATHER...

HAVE RUDOLF FOLLOW YOU AROUND EVERY DAY UNTIL CHRISTMAS

OR...

BE FOLLOWED BY FROSTY THE SNOWMAN

WRAP CHRISTMAS PRESENTS FOR 8 HOURS

OR...

HELP CHILDREN TAKE PICTURES WITH SANTA AT THE MALL

# WOULD YOU RATHER...

7 HOURS OF CHRISTMAS SHOPPING

OR...

10 HOURS OF CHRISTMAS MOVIES

ASK EVERYONE YOU MEET THEIR FAVORITE COLOR

OR...

SMILE REALLY BIG AT EVERYONE AND NOT SAY ANYTHING

# WOULD YOU RATHER...

MAKE SNOW ANGELS

OR...

GO ICE SKATING

---

7 LEVELS OF THE CANDY CANE FOREST

OR...

SEA OF SWIRLY WHIRLY GUMDROPS

### GRINCH

## OR...

### CINDY LOU WHO

### CANDY CANE LEGS

## OR...

### GUM DROPS FOR EYES

# WOULD YOU RATHER...

LARGE ORNAMENTS FOR EARRINGS

OR...

A DECORATED WREATH NECKLACE

SING JINGLE BELLS ONCE EVERY HOUR FOR 2 WEEKS

OR...

WEAR AN ELF COSTUME TO SCHOOL FOR 1 WEEK

# WOULD YOU RATHER...

How the Grinch Stole Christmas

OR...

Christmas Story

Wear a hat made of mistletoe

OR...

wear Jingle Bells on your feet for a week

# WOULD YOU RATHER...

MITTENS FOR HANDS

OR...

SKI'S FOR FEET

---

HAVE YOUR ELF ON A SHELF
TALK TO YOU

OR...

TALK WITH YOUR
CHRISTMAS TREE

# WOULD YOU RATHER...

CHRISTMAS LIGHTS FOR
FINGERNAILS

OR...

SILVER TINSEL FOR HAIR

HOME WITH FAMILY FOR THE
HOLIDAYS

OR...

DISNEYWORLD BY YOURSELF

# WOULD YOU RATHER...

## SING CHRISTMAS CARROLS BY YOURSELF

## OR...

## SIT ON SANTA'S LAP FOR 1 HOUR

## RAKE LEAVES

## OR...

## SHOVEL SNOW

# WOULD YOU RATHER...

Eyes made out of coal

OR...

REINDEER FEET

Spend 11 hours untangling Christmas lights

OR...

Find the one light that is out on a string of Christmas lights a mile long

# WOULD YOU RATHER...

PLAY IN THE SUPER BOWL

OR...

PERFORM IN THE NUTCRACKER

SNOWBALL FOR A HEAD

OR...

100 JINGLE BELLS FOR HAIR

# WOULD YOU RATHER...

SPEND A DAY WITH THE
GRINCH

OR...

SPEND A DAY WITH THE
JACK FROST

GO SLEDDING

OR...

TAKE A HORSE DRAWN
SLEIGH RIDE

# WOULD YOU RATHER...

BUILD A SNOWMAN

OR...

BUILD A SNOW FORT

JUMP IN A **BIG** PILE OF SNOW

OR...

PUDDLE OF RAINWATER

# WOULD YOU RATHER...

THE DAY SLEDDING

OR...

GO SKIING

SLED DOWN A GIANT HILL ONE TIME

OR...

SLED DOWN A SMALL HILL 20 TIMES

# WOULD YOU RATHER...

PLAY IN THE RAIN WITH ELVES

OR...

PLAY IN A SNOW STORM WITH ELVES

SPEND THE NIGHT SLEEPING IN A IGLOO

OR...

SPEND THE NIGHT SLEEPING IN A TENT

# WOULD YOU RATHER...

MAKE PRESENTS FOR YOUR FAMILY INSTEAD OF BUYING THEM

OR...

MAKE ORNAMENTS FOR YOUR CHRISTMAS TREE INSTEAD OF BUYING THEM

HAVE A CHRISTMAS TREE THAT WAS ALREADY CUT DOWN AND DECORATED

OR...

CUT DOWN AND DECORATE IT YOURSELF

# WOULD YOU RATHER...

HAVE A WALK IN THE SNOW

OR...

DRIVE IN THE SNOW

HAVE EGG NOG

OR...

HAVE A HOT COCOA

# WOULD YOU RATHER...

HAVE A SNOW DAY

## OR...

GET DOUBLE PAY

HAVE A CHRISTMAS
VACATION

## OR...

HAVE A SUMMER VACATION

66

HAVE A CHRISTMAS HAM

OR...

HAVE A CHRISTMAS TURKEY

HAVE A REAL CHRISTMAS TREE

OR...

A REUSABLE ONE

# WOULD YOU RATHER...

WRITE A LETTER TO SANTA

OR...

SEND HIM AN EMAIL

DO SECRET SANTA

OR...

RECEIVE A GIFT CARD

# WOULD YOU RATHER...

WATCH THE SANTA PARADE

OR...

WATCH THE CHRISTMAS PARADE

HAVE YOUR FAMILY HOME FOR CHRISTMAS

OR...

AWAY FOR A WEEK OF VACATION

69

# WOULD YOU RATHER...

HAVE CHRISTMAS EVE AT YOUR HOUSE

OR...

SOMEONE ELSE'S HOUSE

LISTEN TO CHRISTMAS SONGS ON THE RADIO

OR...

WATCH CHRISTMAS MOVIES ON TELEVISION

# WOULD YOU RATHER...

HAVE A WHITE CHRISTMAS

OR...

HAVE A GREEN CHRISTMAS

HAVE THE SMELL OF PINE NEEDLES

OR...

THE SMELL OF CINNAMON

# WOULD YOU RATHER...

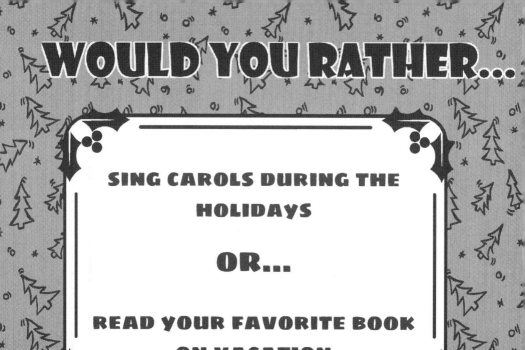

SING CAROLS DURING THE HOLIDAYS

OR...

READ YOUR FAVORITE BOOK ON VACATION

RELIVE A PAST WINTER HOLIDAY AGAIN

OR...

GET TO TRAVEL TO A FUTURE WINTER HOLIDAY

# WOULD YOU RATHER...

**Cook the big Christmas meal every year**

**OR...**

**HAVE TO CLEAN UP AND DO THE DISHES AFTER THE Christmas meal every year**

**Be a kid**

**OR...**

**BE A GRANDPARENT DURING THE HOLIDAYS**

# WOULD YOU RATHER...

GIVE UP ONE FAMILY
CHRISTMAS TRADITION

OR...

START A NEW ONE

WATCH ELF

OR...

WATCH
IT'S A WONDERFUL LIFE

# WOULD YOU RATHER...

WEAR SANTA'S RED SUIT TO SCHOOL

OR...

WEAR A GREEN ELF SUIT TO SCHOOL

SING JINGLE BELLS ONCE EVERY HOUR FOR 2 WEEKS

OR...

WEAR AN ELF COSTUME TO SCHOOL FOR 1 WEEK

# WOULD YOU RATHER...

BE BEST FRIENDS WITH FROSTY THE SNOWMAN

OR...

BE BEST FRIENDS WITH SANTA

HAVE CHRISTMAS LIGHTS FOR FINGERNAILS

OR...

SILVER TINSEL FOR HAIR

# WOULD YOU RATHER...

SING CHRISTMAS CAROLS BY YOURSELF

OR...

SIT ON SANTA'S LAP FOR 1 HOUR

BE AN ELF AT THE NORTH POLE

OR...

ONE OF SANTA'S REINDEER

HAVE EYES MADE OUT OF COAL

OR...

REINDEER FEET

HAVE THE ELF ON THE SHELF BE ALIVE

OR...

HAVE SANTA ACTUALLY IN YOUR BEDROOM WATCHING YOU SLEEP AT NIGHT

SNOWED IN WITH COMPLETE FAMILY DURING THE HOLIDAYS

OR...

ON A BEACH WITH JUST A FEW OF YOUR FAMILY MEMBERS

CHRISTMAS CAROLING

OR...

GO SLEDDING

# WOULD YOU RATHER?
## CHRISTMAS EDITION

**THANK YOU FOR BOUGHT THIS BOOK!**
**LEAVE YOUR REVIEW!**

**YOU ARE THE BEST!**
**I WISH YOU A MERRY CHRISTMAS!**

Made in the USA
Monee, IL
28 November 2022

18774067R00046